# Geography Alive!
## Regions and People

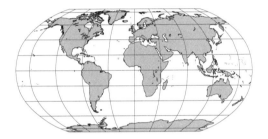

# Mapping Lab
# Manual

**TCi**
Teachers' Curriculum Institute

Director of Development: Liz Russell

Editorial Project Manager: Laura Alavosus

Content Editors: John Bergez, John Burner

Production Editors: Mali Apple, Beverly Cory

Editorial Assistant: Anna Embree

Art Director: John F. Kelly

Production Manager: Lynn Sanchez

Senior Graphic Designer: Christy Uyeno

Graphic Designers: Katy Haun, Paul Rebello, Don Taka

Photo Edit Manager: Margee Robinson

Art Editor: Eric Houts

Audio Director: Katy Haun

**TCi** Teachers' Curriculum Instititute
® P.O. Box 50996
Palo Alto, CA 94303

ISBN13: 978-1-58371-448-5     ISBN10: 1-58371-448-0
5 6 7 8 9 10 -ML- 11 10 09 08

**Program Directors**
Bert Bower
Jim Lobdell

**Program Advisors**
National Council for
Geographic Education

**Curriculum Developers**
Julie Cremin
Erin Fry
Amy George
Colleen Guccione
Steve Seely
Kelly Shafsky
Lisa Sutterer

**Author**
Diane Hart

**Contributing Writers**
Wendy Frey
Erin Fry
Brent Goff
Holly Melton
Hilarie Staton
Ellen Todras
Julie Weiss

**Teacher and Content Consultants**
Melissa Aubuchon
    Indian Trail Middle School
    Plainfield Community Consolidated
    School District 202
    Plainfield, Illinois

Jim Bredin
    Office of the Great Lakes
    Lansing, Michigan

Srinivasan Damodharan
    New Horizon High School
    Bangalore, India

Sarah Giese
    Kenmore Middle School
    Arlington Public Schools
    Arlington, Virginia

Jim Gindling
    Willink Middle School
    Webster Central School District
    Webster, New York

Diana Jordan
    Kenmore Middle School
    Arlington Public Schools
    Arlington, Virginia

Marianne Kenney (NCGE)
    Geography Education Consultant
    Denver, Colorado

Miles Lawrence
    NOAA TPC/National Hurricane
    Center
    Miami, Florida

Patrick McCrystle
    Bellarmine College Preparatory
    San Jose, California

Deanna Morrow
    Martinez Middle School
    Hillsborough County School District
    Lutz, Florida

Michael Radcliffe
    Greenville High School
    Greenville Public Schools
    Greenville, Michigan

Betsy Sheffield
    National Snow and Ice Data Center
    Boulder, Colorado

Stacy Stewart
    NOAA TPC/National Hurricane
    Center
    Miami, Florida

Fred Walk (NCGE)
    Normal Community High School
    McLean County Unit District No. 5
    Normal, Illinois
    Department of Geography
    Illinois State University
    Normal, Illinois

**Scholars**
Dr. Siaw Akwawua
    College of Humanities and
    Social Sciences
    University of Northern Colorado

Dr. Robert Bednarz (NCGE)
    College of Geosciences
    Texas A&M University

Dr. James Dunn (NCGE)
    College of Humanities and
    Social Sciences
    University of Northern Colorado

Dr. Bill Fraser
    Biology Department
    Montana State University

Dr. Patricia Gober (NCGE)
    Department of Geography
    Arizona State University

Dr. Susan Hardwick (NCGE)
Department of Geography
University of Oregon

Professor Gail Hobbs (NCGE)
Department of Anthropological
and Geographical Sciences
Los Angeles Pierce College

Dr. Phil Klein (NCGE)
College of Humanities and
Social Sciences
University of Northern Colorado

Dr. Gwenda Rice (NCGE)
College of Education
Western Oregon University

Dr. Kit Salter (retired; NCGE)
Department of Geography
University of Missouri

Dr. Earl Scott (retired)
Department of Geography
University of Minnesota

**Music Consultant**
Melanie Pinkert
Music Faculty
Montgomery College, Maryland

**Geography Specialist**
Mapping Specialists
Madison, Wisconsin

**Internet Consultant**
Clinton Couse
Educational Technology Consultant
Seattle, Washington

**Researcher**
Jessica Efron
Library Faculty
Appalachian State University

# Contents

# Canada and
# the United States

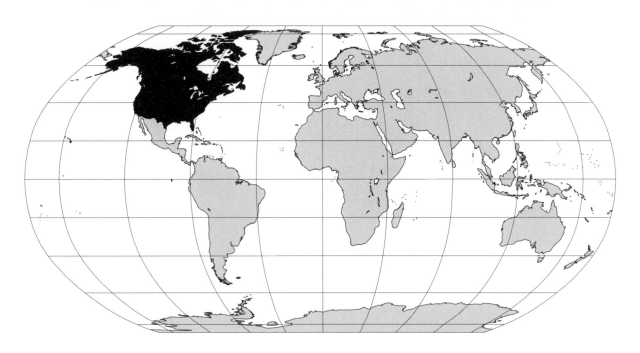

## Preview
# Making a Mental Map of the Region

Draw an outline map of Canada and the United States on the next page or on a separate sheet of paper. Add a compass rose to your map, showing where north, south, east, and west are. Then draw and label these features where you think they are located:

- the Arctic Circle

- two large bodies of water that are not oceans

- a mountain range

- a large river

- the political boundaries of the two countries in this region

- political boundaries for any states, provinces, or territories you think you know

Draw your mental map of Canada and the United States below.

## Challenge 1
### Learning About the Physical Geography of Canada and the United States

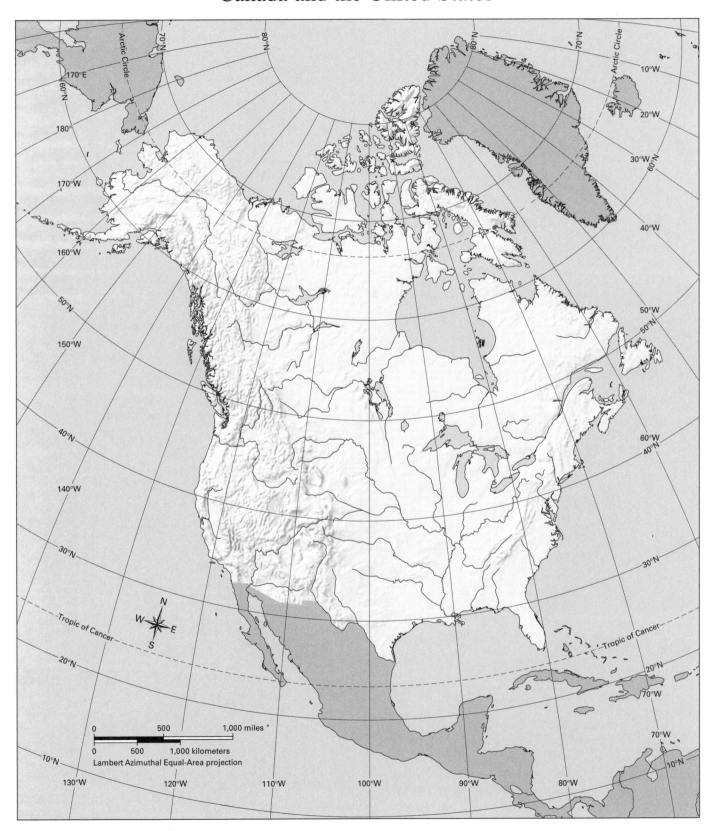

## Challenge 2
## Learning About the Human Geography of
## Canada and the United States

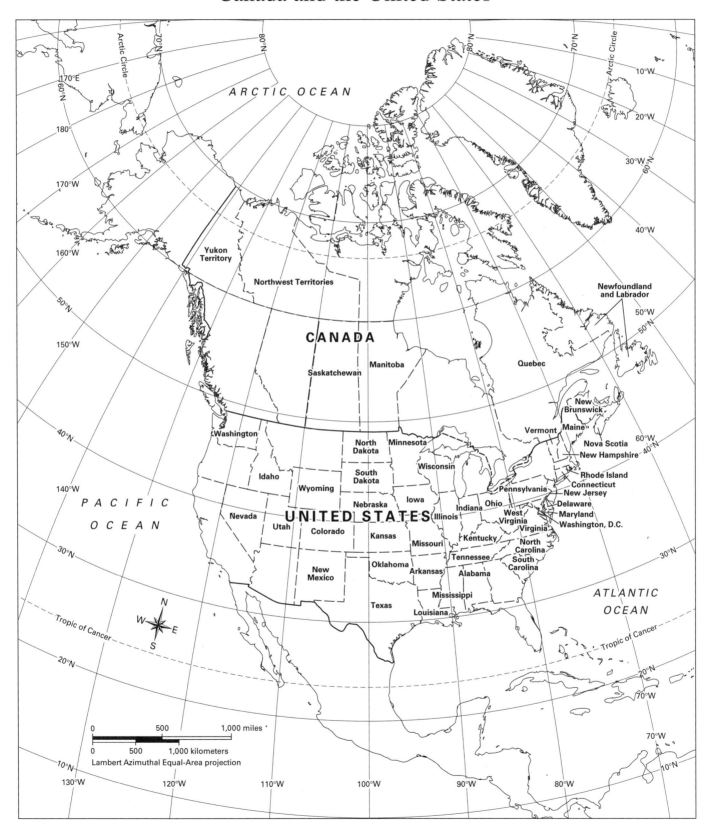

## Challenge 3
## Using Geography Skills to Answer "Where?"

| Question | Circle the thematic map you used. Then answer the question in complete sentences. | | | | |
|---|---|---|---|---|---|
| 1 | Physical Features | Climate Zones | Vegetation Zones | Population Density | Economic Activity |
| 2 | Physical Features | Climate Zones | Vegetation Zones | Population Density | Economic Activity |
| 3 | Physical Features | Climate Zones | Vegetation Zones | Population Density | Economic Activity |
| 4 | Physical Features | Climate Zones | Vegetation Zones | Population Density | Economic Activity |
| 5 | Physical Features | Climate Zones | Vegetation Zones | Population Density | Economic Activity |
| 6 | Physical Features | Climate Zones | Vegetation Zones | Population Density | Economic Activity |
| 7 | Physical Features | Climate Zones | Vegetation Zones | Population Density | Economic Activity |
| 8 | Physical Features | Climate Zones | Vegetation Zones | Population Density | Economic Activity |
| 9 | Physical Features | Climate Zones | Vegetation Zones | Population Density | Economic Activity |
| 10 | Physical Features | Climate Zones | Vegetation Zones | Population Density | Economic Activity |

**Challenge 4**
## Using Geography Skills to Answer "Why There?"

| Question | Circle the thematic maps you used. Then answer the question in complete sentences. | | | | |
|---|---|---|---|---|---|
| 1 | Physical Features | Climate Zones | Vegetation Zones | Population Density | Economic Activity |
| 2 | Physical Features | Climate Zones | Vegetation Zones | Population Density | Economic Activity |
| 3 | Physical Features | Climate Zones | Vegetation Zones | Population Density | Economic Activity |
| 4 | Physical Features | Climate Zones | Vegetation Zones | Population Density | Economic Activity |
| 5 | Physical Features | Climate Zones | Vegetation Zones | Population Density | Economic Activity |
| 6 | Physical Features | Climate Zones | Vegetation Zones | Population Density | Economic Activity |

## Challenge 5
## Using Maps to Analyze a Field Photograph

| | **Location A**<br>(40° north, 74° west) | **Location B**<br>(76° north, 80° west) | **Location C**<br>(60° north, 147° west) |
|---|---|---|---|
| **Physical Features** | | | |
| **Climate Zones** | | | |
| **Vegetation Zones** | | | |
| **Population Density** | | | |
| **Economic Activity** | | | |

## Challenge 5
# Using Maps to Analyze a Field Photograph

We think the field photograph best matches Location _____ .

**Supporting-Evidence Statements**

**1.** From the _____ map, we learned that this location

_____

_____ .

In the field photograph, we see _____

_____

_____ .


**2.** From the _____ map, we learned that this location

_____

_____ .

In the field photograph, we see _____

_____

_____ .


**3.** From the _____ map, we learned that this location

_____

_____ .

In the field photograph, we see _____

_____

_____ .


**4.** From the _____ map, we learned that this location

_____

_____ .

In the field photograph, we see _____

_____

_____ .

# Latin America

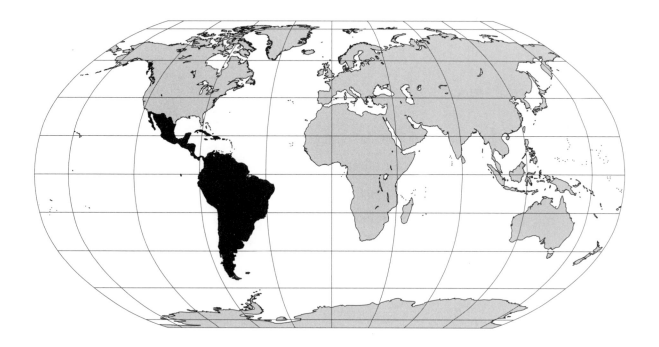

**Preview**

# Making a Mental Map of the Region

Draw an outline map of Latin America on the next page or on a separate sheet of paper. Add a compass rose to your map, showing where north, south, east, and west are. Then draw and label these features where you think they are located:

- the equator
- other regions or bodies of water that you think lie north, south, east, and west of this region
- the area(s) that you think have a humid, tropical climate
- the area(s) that you think have a cold, polar climate
- the area(s) that you think have the greatest population
- the area(s) that you think have the least population

Draw your mental map of Latin America below.

## Challenge 1
## Learning About the Physical Geography
## of Latin America

## Challenge 2
## Learning About the Human Geography
## of Latin America

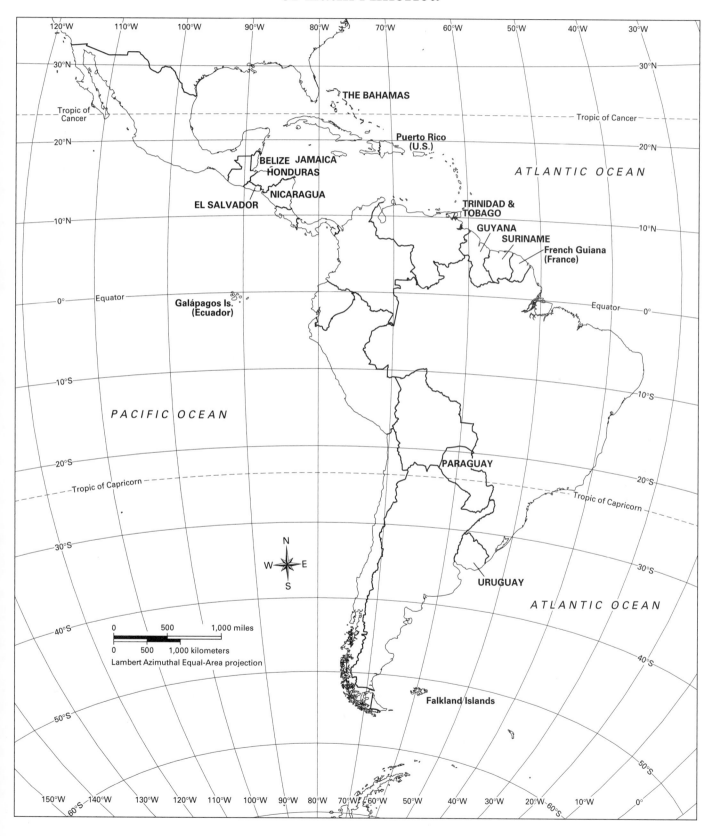

## Challenge 3
## Using Geography Skills to Answer "Where?"

| Question | Circle the thematic map you used. Then answer the question in complete sentences. | | | | |
|---|---|---|---|---|---|
| 1 | Physical Features | Climate Zones | Vegetation Zones | Population Density | Economic Activity |
| 2 | Physical Features | Climate Zones | Vegetation Zones | Population Density | Economic Activity |
| 3 | Physical Features | Climate Zones | Vegetation Zones | Population Density | Economic Activity |
| 4 | Physical Features | Climate Zones | Vegetation Zones | Population Density | Economic Activity |
| 5 | Physical Features | Climate Zones | Vegetation Zones | Population Density | Economic Activity |
| 6 | Physical Features | Climate Zones | Vegetation Zones | Population Density | Economic Activity |
| 7 | Physical Features | Climate Zones | Vegetation Zones | Population Density | Economic Activity |
| 8 | Physical Features | Climate Zones | Vegetation Zones | Population Density | Economic Activity |
| 9 | Physical Features | Climate Zones | Vegetation Zones | Population Density | Economic Activity |
| 10 | Physical Features | Climate Zones | Vegetation Zones | Population Density | Economic Activity |

## Challenge 4
## Using Geography Skills to Answer "Why There?"

| Question | Circle the thematic maps you used. Then answer the question in complete sentences. | | | | |
|---|---|---|---|---|---|
| 1 | Physical Features | Climate Zones | Vegetation Zones | Population Density | Economic Activity |
| 2 | Physical Features | Climate Zones | Vegetation Zones | Population Density | Economic Activity |
| 3 | Physical Features | Climate Zones | Vegetation Zones | Population Density | Economic Activity |
| 4 | Physical Features | Climate Zones | Vegetation Zones | Population Density | Economic Activity |
| 5 | Physical Features | Climate Zones | Vegetation Zones | Population Density | Economic Activity |
| 6 | Physical Features | Climate Zones | Vegetation Zones | Population Density | Economic Activity |

## Challenge 5
## Using Maps to Analyze a Field Photograph

|  | Location A (27° north, 105° west) | Location B (3° south, 65° west) | Location C (15° south, 72° west) |
|---|---|---|---|
| **Physical Features** |  |  |  |
| **Climate Zones** |  |  |  |
| **Vegetation Zones** |  |  |  |
| **Population Density** |  |  |  |
| **Economic Activity** |  |  |  |

### Challenge 5
# Using Maps to Analyze a Field Photograph

We think the field photograph best matches Location _____ .

**Supporting-Evidence Statements**

**1.** From the _____ map, we learned that this location

_____

_____ .

In the field photograph, we see _____

_____

_____ .

**2.** From the _____ map, we learned that this location

_____

_____ .

In the field photograph, we see _____

_____

_____ .

**3.** From the _____ map, we learned that this location

_____

_____ .

In the field photograph, we see _____

_____

_____ .

**4.** From the _____ map, we learned that this location

_____

_____ .

In the field photograph, we see _____

_____

_____ .

# Europe and Russia

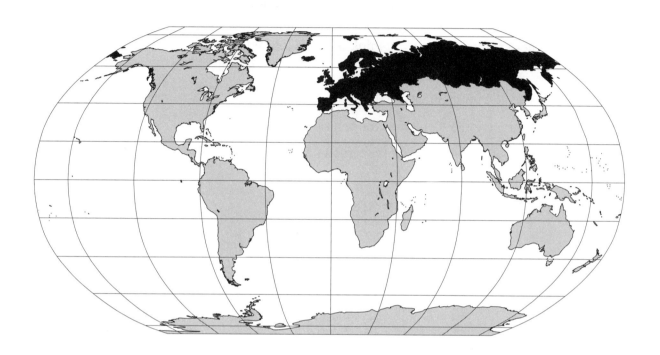

**Preview**

# Making a Mental Map of the Region

## Part 1

Look at the unfinished outline map of Europe on the next page. Add a compass rose to the map, showing where north, south, east, and west are. Then draw and label these features where you think they are located:

- the prime meridian

- the British Isles, Spain and Portugal, and Italy

- political boundaries for any other countries you think you know

- the ocean that lies west of this region, and the large body of water that lies south of this region

- any European cities you think you know

## Part 2

Look at the outline map of Russia on the next page. Add a compass rose to the map. Then draw and label these features where you think they are located:

- the Arctic Circle

- the ocean that lies north of this region

- any area(s) that you think have a cold, polar climate

- any Russian cities you think you know

Add details to the outlines below based on your mental map of the region.

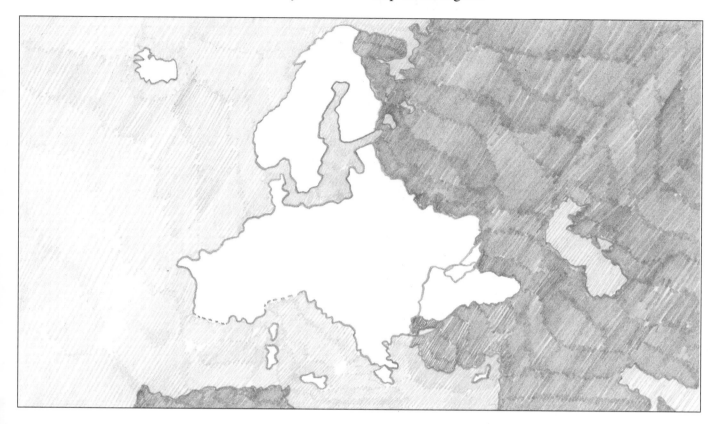

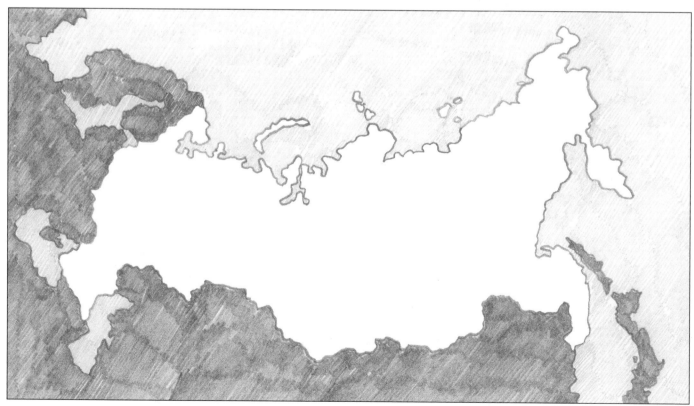

## Challenge 1
## Learning About the Physical Geography
## of Europe and Russia

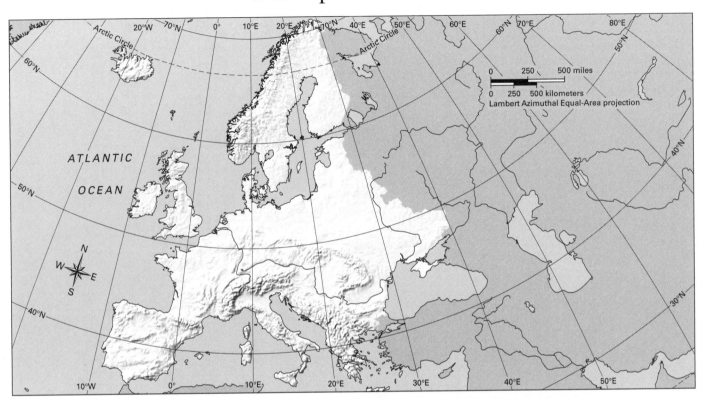

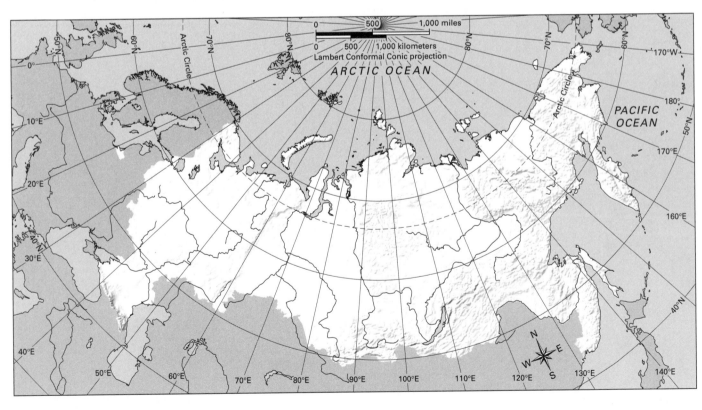

## Challenge 2
# Learning About the Human Geography
# of Europe and Russia

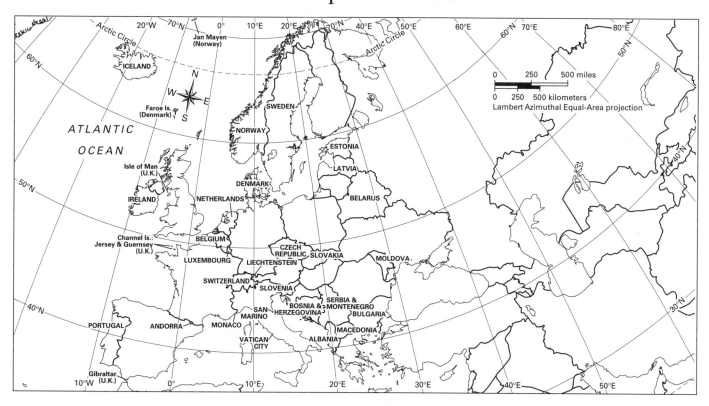

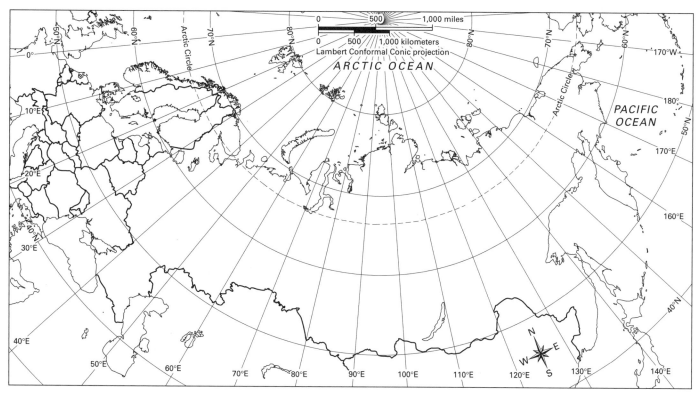

## Challenge 3
## Using Geography Skills to Answer "Where?"

| Question | Circle the thematic map you used. Then answer the question in complete sentences. | | | | |
|---|---|---|---|---|---|
| 1 | Physical Features | Climate Zones | Vegetation Zones | Population Density | Economic Activity |
| 2 | Physical Features | Climate Zones | Vegetation Zones | Population Density | Economic Activity |
| 3 | Physical Features | Climate Zones | Vegetation Zones | Population Density | Economic Activity |
| 4 | Physical Features | Climate Zones | Vegetation Zones | Population Density | Economic Activity |
| 5 | Physical Features | Climate Zones | Vegetation Zones | Population Density | Economic Activity |
| 6 | Physical Features | Climate Zones | Vegetation Zones | Population Density | Economic Activity |
| 7 | Physical Features | Climate Zones | Vegetation Zones | Population Density | Economic Activity |
| 8 | Physical Features | Climate Zones | Vegetation Zones | Population Density | Economic Activity |
| 9 | Physical Features | Climate Zones | Vegetation Zones | Population Density | Economic Activity |
| 10 | Physical Features | Climate Zones | Vegetation Zones | Population Density | Economic Activity |

## Challenge 4
## Using Geography Skills to Answer "Why There?"

| Question | Circle the thematic maps you used. Then answer the question in complete sentences. | | | | |
|---|---|---|---|---|---|
| 1 | Physical Features | Climate Zones | Vegetation Zones | Population Density | Economic Activity |
| 2 | Physical Features | Climate Zones | Vegetation Zones | Population Density | Economic Activity |
| 3 | Physical Features | Climate Zones | Vegetation Zones | Population Density | Economic Activity |
| 4 | Physical Features | Climate Zones | Vegetation Zones | Population Density | Economic Activity |
| 5 | Physical Features | Climate Zones | Vegetation Zones | Population Density | Economic Activity |
| 6 | Physical Features | Climate Zones | Vegetation Zones | Population Density | Economic Activity |

**Challenge 5**
## Using Maps to Analyze a Field Photograph

| | Location A (66° north, 25° east) | Location B (57° north, 22° east) | Location C (67° north, 79° east) |
|---|---|---|---|
| **Physical Features** | | | |
| **Climate Zones** | | | |
| **Vegetation Zones** | | | |
| **Population Density** | | | |
| **Economic Activity** | | | |

## Challenge 5
## Using Maps to Analyze a Field Photograph

We think the field photograph best matches Location _____ .

**Supporting-Evidence Statements**

**1.** From the _____ map, we learned that this location

_____

_____ .

In the field photograph, we see _____

_____

_____ .

**2.** From the _____ map, we learned that this location

_____

_____ .

In the field photograph, we see _____

_____

_____ .

**3.** From the _____ map, we learned that this location

_____

_____ .

In the field photograph, we see _____

_____

_____ .

**4.** From the _____ map, we learned that this location

_____

_____ .

In the field photograph, we see _____

_____

_____ .

# Africa

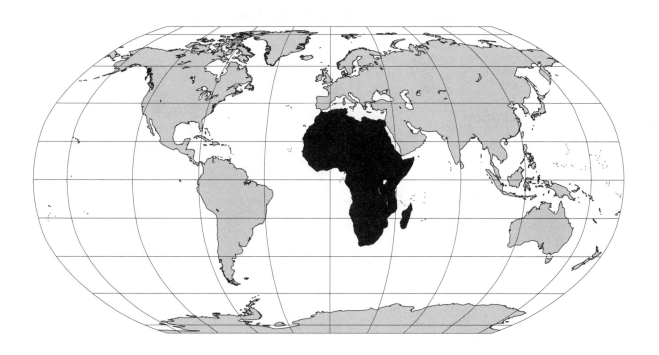

**Preview**

## Making a Mental Map of the Region

Draw an outline map of Africa on the next page or on a separate sheet
of paper. Add a compass rose to your map, showing where north, south,
east, and west are. Then draw and label these features where you think
they are located:

- the equator

- the prime meridian

- the highest mountain in Africa

- two long rivers

- a desert area

- any countries you think you know

Draw your mental map of Africa below.

## Challenge 1
## Learning About the Physical Geography
## of Africa

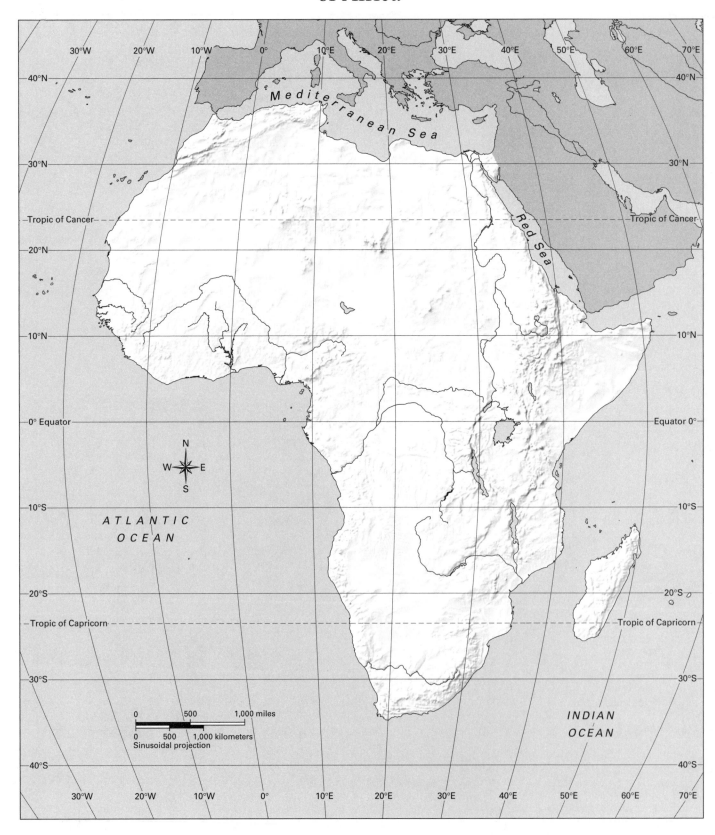

## Challenge 2
## Learning About the Human Geography
## of Africa

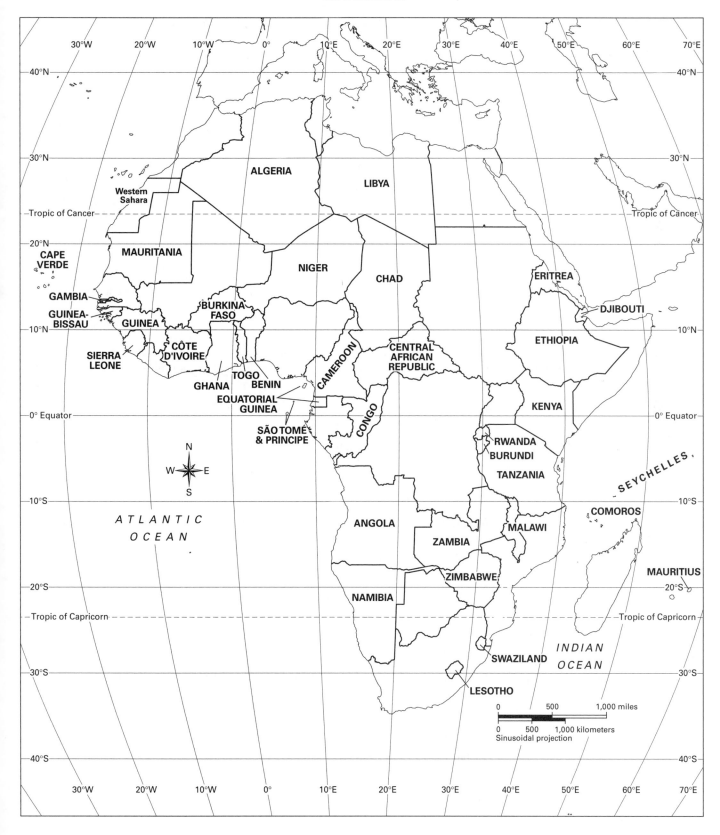

### Challenge 3
## Using Geography Skills to Answer "Where?"

| Question | Circle the thematic map you used. Then answer the question in complete sentences. | | | | |
|---|---|---|---|---|---|
| 1 | Physical Features | Climate Zones | Vegetation Zones | Population Density | Economic Activity |
| 2 | Physical Features | Climate Zones | Vegetation Zones | Population Density | Economic Activity |
| 3 | Physical Features | Climate Zones | Vegetation Zones | Population Density | Economic Activity |
| 4 | Physical Features | Climate Zones | Vegetation Zones | Population Density | Economic Activity |
| 5 | Physical Features | Climate Zones | Vegetation Zones | Population Density | Economic Activity |
| 6 | Physical Features | Climate Zones | Vegetation Zones | Population Density | Economic Activity |
| 7 | Physical Features | Climate Zones | Vegetation Zones | Population Density | Economic Activity |
| 8 | Physical Features | Climate Zones | Vegetation Zones | Population Density | Economic Activity |
| 9 | Physical Features | Climate Zones | Vegetation Zones | Population Density | Economic Activity |
| 10 | Physical Features | Climate Zones | Vegetation Zones | Population Density | Economic Activity |

**Challenge 4**

## Using Geography Skills to Answer "Why There?"

| Question | Circle the thematic maps you used. Then answer the question in complete sentences. | | | | |
|----------|------------------|-------------|-----------------|-------------------|-------------------|
| 1 | Physical Features | Climate Zones | Vegetation Zones | Population Density | Economic Activity |
| 2 | Physical Features | Climate Zones | Vegetation Zones | Population Density | Economic Activity |
| 3 | Physical Features | Climate Zones | Vegetation Zones | Population Density | Economic Activity |
| 4 | Physical Features | Climate Zones | Vegetation Zones | Population Density | Economic Activity |
| 5 | Physical Features | Climate Zones | Vegetation Zones | Population Density | Economic Activity |
| 6 | Physical Features | Climate Zones | Vegetation Zones | Population Density | Economic Activity |

**Challenge 5**
## Using Maps to Analyze a Field Photograph

| | Location A (13° north, 6° west) | Location B (30° south, 29° east) | Location C (28° north, 31° east) |
|---|---|---|---|
| **Physical Features** | | | |
| **Climate Zones** | | | |
| **Vegetation Zones** | | | |
| **Population Density** | | | |
| **Economic Activity** | | | |

## Challenge 5
## Using Maps to Analyze a Field Photograph

We think the field photograph best matches Location _____ .

**Supporting-Evidence Statements**

**1.** From the _____ map, we learned that this location

_____

_____ .

In the field photograph, we see _____

_____

_____ .


**2.** From the _____ map, we learned that this location

_____

_____ .

In the field photograph, we see _____

_____

_____ .


**3.** From the _____ map, we learned that this location

_____

_____ .

In the field photograph, we see _____

_____

_____ .


**4.** From the _____ map, we learned that this location

_____

_____ .

In the field photograph, we see _____

_____

_____ .

# Southwest and
# Central Asia

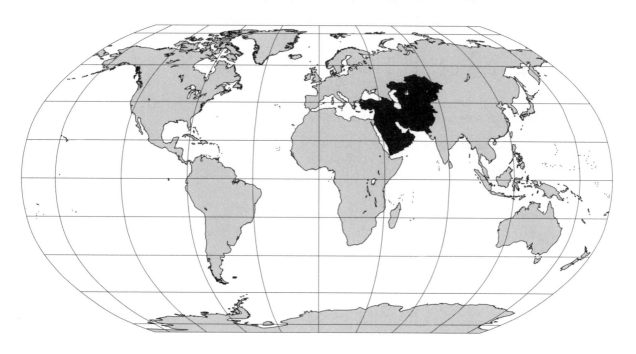

**Preview**

## Making a Mental Map of the Region

Look at the outline map of Central and Southwest Asia on the next page. Add a compass rose to the map, showing where north, south, east, and west are. Then draw and label these features where you think they are located:

- at least two physical features (these could be mountains, rivers, lakes, or deserts)

- the other regions and the seas or gulfs that border this region

- the boundaries of any countries you think you know

- any area that you think has a very dry (arid) climate

- any area that you think is densely populated

Add details to the outline below based on your mental map of the region.

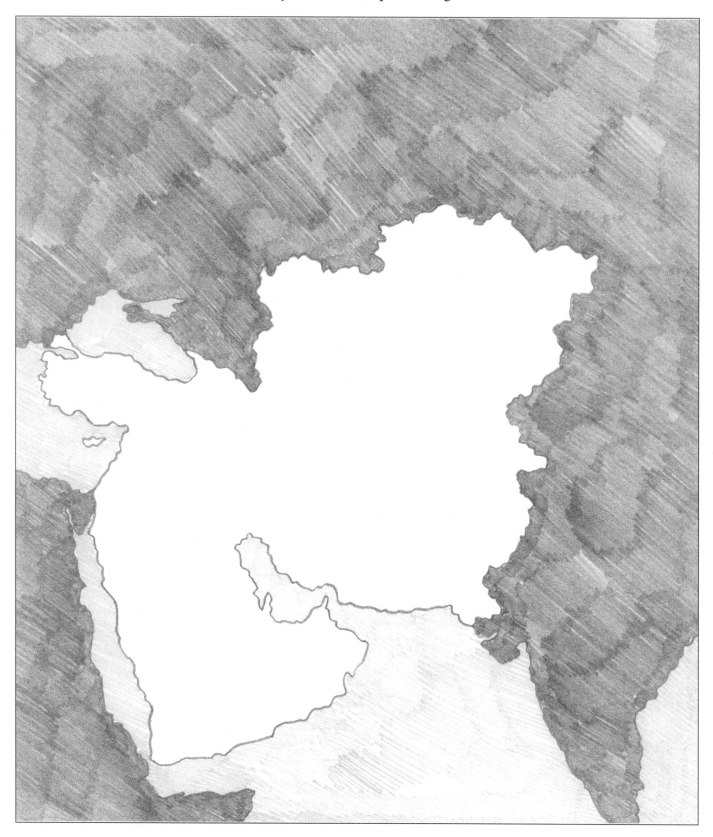

## Challenge 1
## Learning About the Physical Geography
## of Southwest and Central Asia

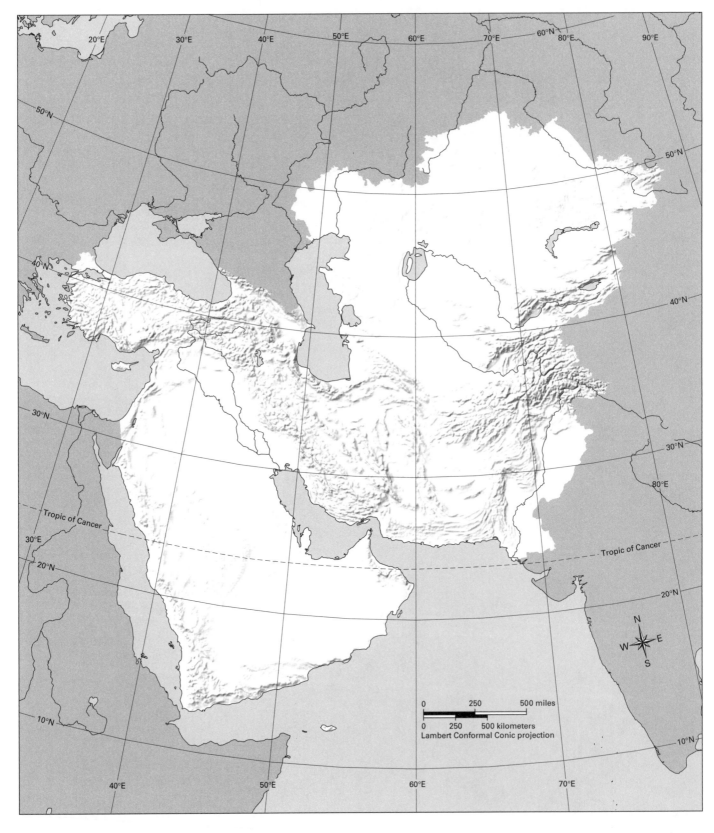

## Challenge 2
## Learning About the Human Geography
## of Southwest and Central Asia

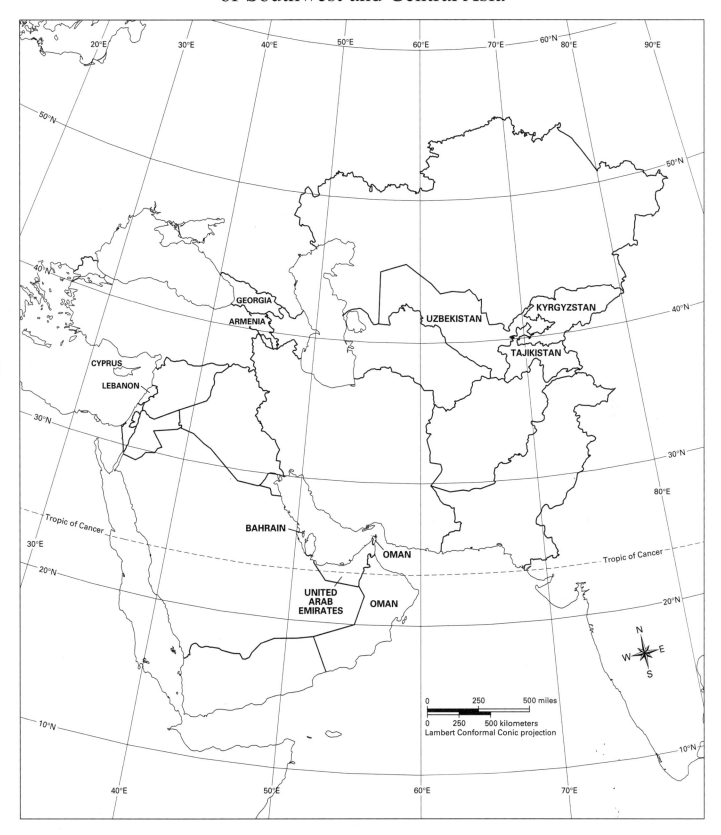

## Challenge 3
## Using Geography Skills to Answer "Where?"

| Question | Circle the thematic map you used. Then answer the question in complete sentences. | | | | |
|---|---|---|---|---|---|
| 1 | Physical Features | Climate Zones | Vegetation Zones | Population Density | Economic Activity |
| 2 | Physical Features | Climate Zones | Vegetation Zones | Population Density | Economic Activity |
| 3 | Physical Features | Climate Zones | Vegetation Zones | Population Density | Economic Activity |
| 4 | Physical Features | Climate Zones | Vegetation Zones | Population Density | Economic Activity |
| 5 | Physical Features | Climate Zones | Vegetation Zones | Population Density | Economic Activity |
| 6 | Physical Features | Climate Zones | Vegetation Zones | Population Density | Economic Activity |
| 7 | Physical Features | Climate Zones | Vegetation Zones | Population Density | Economic Activity |
| 8 | Physical Features | Climate Zones | Vegetation Zones | Population Density | Economic Activity |
| 9 | Physical Features | Climate Zones | Vegetation Zones | Population Density | Economic Activity |
| 10 | Physical Features | Climate Zones | Vegetation Zones | Population Density | Economic Activity |

## Challenge 4
## Using Geography Skills to Answer "Why There?"

| Question | Circle the thematic maps you used. Then answer the question in complete sentences. | | | | |
|---|---|---|---|---|---|
| 1 | Physical Features | Climate Zones | Vegetation Zones | Population Density | Economic Activity |
| 2 | Physical Features | Climate Zones | Vegetation Zones | Population Density | Economic Activity |
| 3 | Physical Features | Climate Zones | Vegetation Zones | Population Density | Economic Activity |
| 4 | Physical Features | Climate Zones | Vegetation Zones | Population Density | Economic Activity |
| 5 | Physical Features | Climate Zones | Vegetation Zones | Population Density | Economic Activity |
| 6 | Physical Features | Climate Zones | Vegetation Zones | Population Density | Economic Activity |

**Challenge 5**

## Using Maps to Analyze a Field Photograph

| | Location A (22° north, 48° east) | Location B (34° north, 50° east) | Location C (25° north, 67° east) |
|---|---|---|---|
| **Physical Features** | | | |
| **Climate Zones** | | | |
| **Vegetation Zones** | | | |
| **Population Density** | | | |
| **Economic Activity** | | | |

## Challenge 5
## Using Maps to Analyze a Field Photograph

We think the field photograph best matches Location _____ .

**Supporting-Evidence Statements**

**1.** From the _____ map, we learned that this location

_____

_____ .

In the field photograph, we see _____

_____

_____ .

**2.** From the _____ map, we learned that this location

_____

_____ .

In the field photograph, we see _____

_____

_____ .

**3.** From the _____ map, we learned that this location

_____

_____ .

In the field photograph, we see _____

_____

_____ .

**4.** From the _____ map, we learned that this location

_____

_____ .

In the field photograph, we see _____

_____

_____ .

# Monsoon Asia

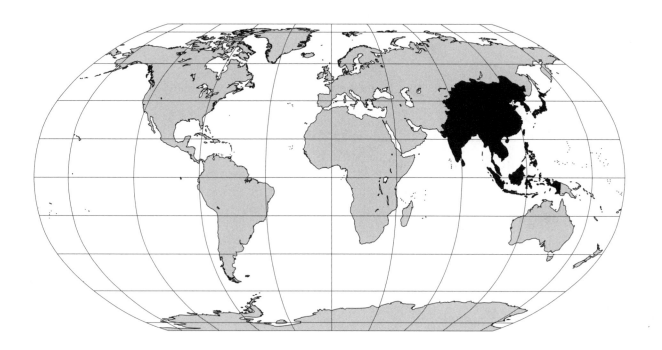

**Preview**
# Making a Mental Map of the Region

Look at the outline map of Monsoon Asia on the next page. Add a
compass rose to the map, showing where north, south, east, and west
are. Then draw or shade and label these features where you think they
are located:

- the equator
- the other regions and bodies of water that lie to the north, south, east,
  and west
- the missing islands of Sri Lanka, Taiwan, and Japan
- the area(s) that have a tropical wet climate
- the area(s) that have a dry (arid or semiarid) climate
- the area(s) that have the greatest population
- the area(s) that have the least population

Add details to the outline below based on your mental map of the region.

## Challenge 1
## Learning About the Physical Geography
## of Monsoon Asia

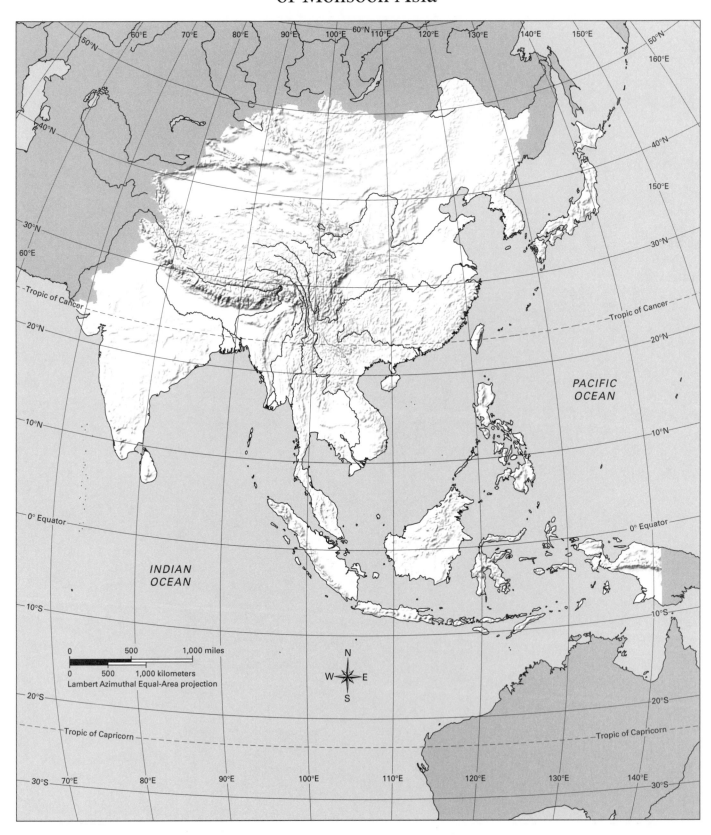

## Challenge 2
## Learning About the Human Geography
## of Monsoon Asia

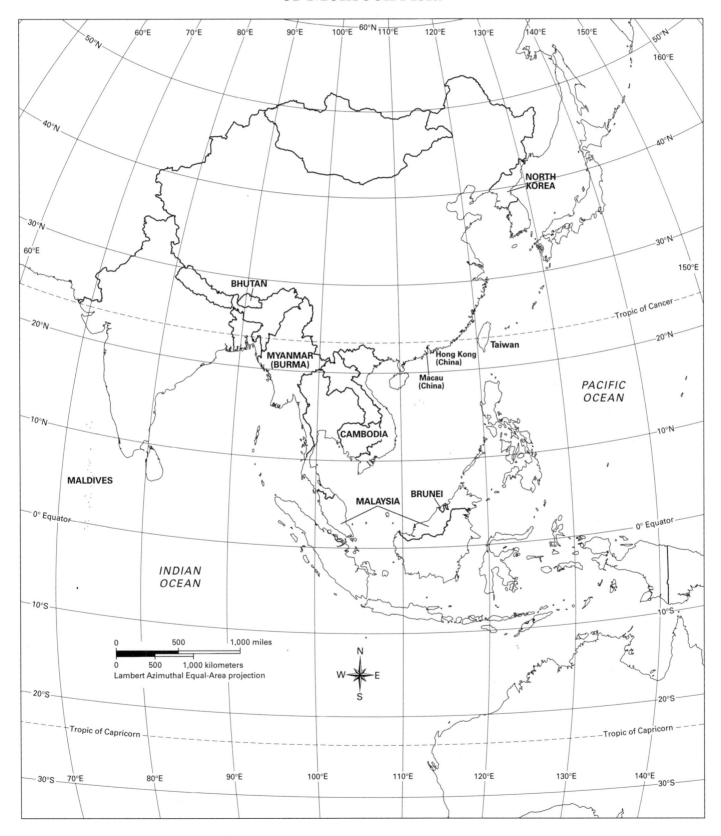

NORTH
KOREA

Tropic of Cancer

BHUTAN

Hong Kong
(China)

Taiwan

MYANMAR
(BURMA)

Macau
(China)

PACIFIC
OCEAN

CAMBODIA

MALDIVES

BRUNEI

MALAYSIA

0° Equator

0° Equator

INDIAN
OCEAN

1,000 miles

0      500

0      500   1,000 kilometers
Lambert Azimuthal Equal-Area projection

N
W · E
S

Tropic of Capricorn

Tropic of Capricorn

## Challenge 3
## Using Geography Skills to Answer "Where?"

| Question | Circle the thematic map you used. Then answer the question in complete sentences. | | | | |
|---|---|---|---|---|---|
| 1 | Physical Features | Climate Zones | Vegetation Zones | Population Density | Economic Activity |
| 2 | Physical Features | Climate Zones | Vegetation Zones | Population Density | Economic Activity |
| 3 | Physical Features | Climate Zones | Vegetation Zones | Population Density | Economic Activity |
| 4 | Physical Features | Climate Zones | Vegetation Zones | Population Density | Economic Activity |
| 5 | Physical Features | Climate Zones | Vegetation Zones | Population Density | Economic Activity |
| 6 | Physical Features | Climate Zones | Vegetation Zones | Population Density | Economic Activity |
| 7 | Physical Features | Climate Zones | Vegetation Zones | Population Density | Economic Activity |
| 8 | Physical Features | Climate Zones | Vegetation Zones | Population Density | Economic Activity |
| 9 | Physical Features | Climate Zones | Vegetation Zones | Population Density | Economic Activity |
| 10 | Physical Features | Climate Zones | Vegetation Zones | Population Density | Economic Activity |

## Challenge 4
## Using Geography Skills to Answer "Why There?"

| Question | Circle the thematic maps you used. Then answer the question in complete sentences. | | | | |
|---|---|---|---|---|---|
| 1 | Physical Features | Climate Zones | Vegetation Zones | Population Density | Economic Activity |
| 2 | Physical Features | Climate Zones | Vegetation Zones | Population Density | Economic Activity |
| 3 | Physical Features | Climate Zones | Vegetation Zones | Population Density | Economic Activity |
| 4 | Physical Features | Climate Zones | Vegetation Zones | Population Density | Economic Activity |
| 5 | Physical Features | Climate Zones | Vegetation Zones | Population Density | Economic Activity |
| 6 | Physical Features | Climate Zones | Vegetation Zones | Population Density | Economic Activity |

## Challenge 5
## Using Maps to Analyze a Field Photograph

|  | **Location A**<br>(40° north, 85° east) | **Location B**<br>(4° south, 138° east) | **Location C**<br>(19° north, 73° east) |
|---|---|---|---|
| **Physical Features** |  |  |  |
| **Climate Zones** |  |  |  |
| **Vegetation Zones** |  |  |  |
| **Population Density** |  |  |  |
| **Economic Activity** |  |  |  |

## Challenge 5
## Using Maps to Analyze a Field Photograph

We think the field photograph best matches Location _____ .

### Supporting-Evidence Statements

**1.** From the _____ map, we learned that this location

_____

_____ .

In the field photograph, we see _____

_____

_____ .

**2.** From the _____ map, we learned that this location

_____

_____ .

In the field photograph, we see _____

_____

_____ .

**3.** From the _____ map, we learned that this location

_____

_____ .

In the field photograph, we see _____

_____

_____ .

**4.** From the _____ map, we learned that this location

_____

_____ .

In the field photograph, we see _____

_____

_____ .

# Oceania and Antarctica

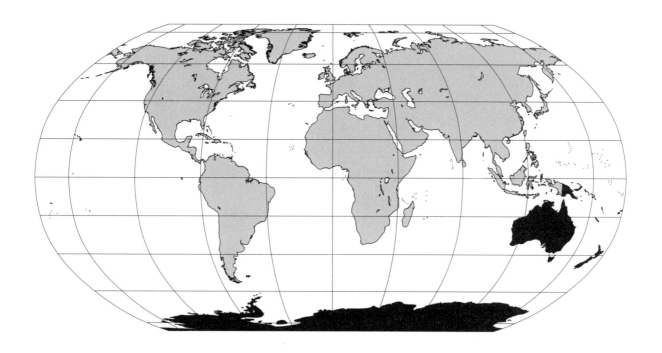

**Preview**

## Making a Mental Map of the Region

Look at the unfinished outline map of Oceania and Antarctica on the next page. Add a compass rose to the map, showing where north, south, east, and west are. Then draw or shade and label these features where you think they are located:

- Australia and New Zealand

- Antarctica

- the equator

- the oceans

- the areas that you think have the greatest population

- the areas that you think have the least population

Add details to the outline below based on your mental map of the region.

## Challenge 1
## Learning About the Physical Geography
## of Oceania and Antarctica

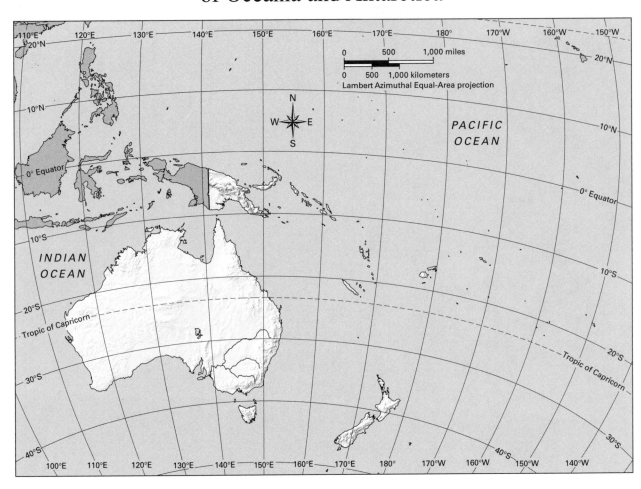

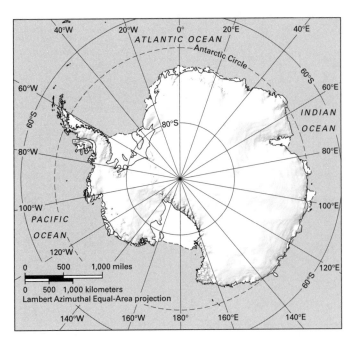

## Challenge 2
## Learning About the Human Geography
## of Oceania and Antarctica

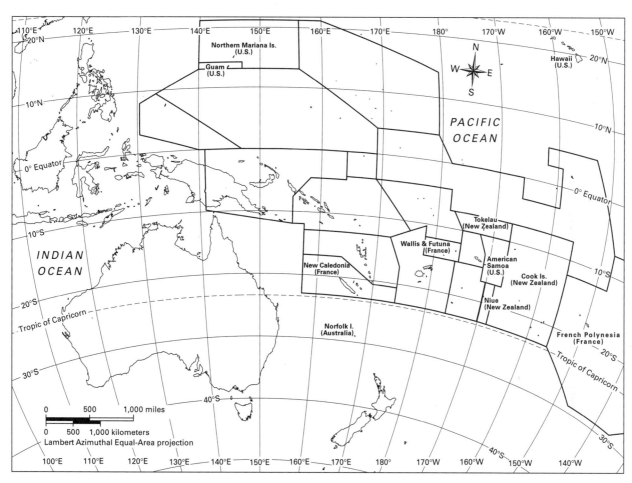

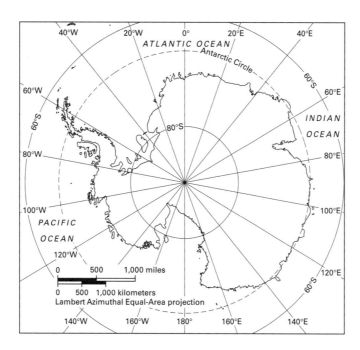

## Challenge 3
## Using Geography Skills to Answer "Where?"

| Question | Circle the thematic map you used. Then answer the question in complete sentences. | | | | |
|---|---|---|---|---|---|
| 1 | Physical Features | Climate Zones | Vegetation Zones | Population Density | Economic Activity |
| 2 | Physical Features | Climate Zones | Vegetation Zones | Population Density | Economic Activity |
| 3 | Physical Features | Climate Zones | Vegetation Zones | Population Density | Economic Activity |
| 4 | Physical Features | Climate Zones | Vegetation Zones | Population Density | Economic Activity |
| 5 | Physical Features | Climate Zones | Vegetation Zones | Population Density | Economic Activity |
| 6 | Physical Features | Climate Zones | Vegetation Zones | Population Density | Economic Activity |
| 7 | Physical Features | Climate Zones | Vegetation Zones | Population Density | Economic Activity |
| 8 | Physical Features | Climate Zones | Vegetation Zones | Population Density | Economic Activity |
| 9 | Physical Features | Climate Zones | Vegetation Zones | Population Density | Economic Activity |
| 10 | Physical Features | Climate Zones | Vegetation Zones | Population Density | Economic Activity |

## Challenge 4
## Using Geography Skills to Answer "Why There?"

| Question | Circle the thematic maps you used. Then answer the question in complete sentences. | | | | |
|---|---|---|---|---|---|
| 1 | Physical Features | Climate Zones | Vegetation Zones | Population Density | Economic Activity |
| 2 | Physical Features | Climate Zones | Vegetation Zones | Population Density | Economic Activity |
| 3 | Physical Features | Climate Zones | Vegetation Zones | Population Density | Economic Activity |
| 4 | Physical Features | Climate Zones | Vegetation Zones | Population Density | Economic Activity |
| 5 | Physical Features | Climate Zones | Vegetation Zones | Population Density | Economic Activity |
| 6 | Physical Features | Climate Zones | Vegetation Zones | Population Density | Economic Activity |

## Challenge 5
## Using Maps to Analyze a Field Photograph

| | Location A (32° south, 130° east) | Location B (7° north, 152° east) | Location C (37° south, 174° east) |
|---|---|---|---|
| **Physical Features** | | | |
| **Climate Zones** | | | |
| **Vegetation Zones** | | | |
| **Population Density** | | | |
| **Economic Activity** | | | |

## Challenge 5
# Using Maps to Analyze a Field Photograph

We think the field photograph best matches Location _____ .

**Supporting-Evidence Statements**

**1.** From the _____ map, we learned that this location

_____

_____ .

In the field photograph, we see _____

_____

_____ .

**2.** From the _____ map, we learned that this location

_____

_____ .

In the field photograph, we see _____

_____

_____ .

**3.** From the _____ map, we learned that this location

_____

_____ .

In the field photograph, we see _____

_____

_____ .

**4.** From the _____ map, we learned that this location

_____

_____ .

In the field photograph, we see _____

_____

_____ .